BRIGHT IDEAS—Problem Solving, Gr. 4-8

This calendar makes learning fun. Because the activities are quick and require few materials, they are the perfect way to turn extra classroom minutes into educational experiences. Help students improve their problem-solving skills through exercises in math, storytelling, writing, interpretation, and more! The ideas are wonderful for use in a whole language or cooperative learning setting, and can be used year after year.

Note: You may need to adapt some activities to meet the specific needs of your group.

Project Editor: Peggy Hapke Lewis

Y0-BVQ-959

Bright Ideas Calendars

Science, Gr. 4–8

Problem Solving, Gr. 4–8

Social Studies, Gr. 4–8

Mathematics, Gr. 4–8

Geography, Gr. 4–8

Spelling & Grammar, Gr. 4–8

Poetry, Gr. 4–8

Language Arts, Gr. 4–8

Self-Concept, Gr. 4–8

Vocabulary, Gr. 4–8

Multicultural, Gr. 4–8

Creative Thinking, Gr. 4–8

Writing, Gr. 4–8

Trivia, Gr. 4–8

McDonald Publishing Co.
567 Hanley Industrial Court
St. Louis, MO 63144-1901

January 1

Make as many words as you can from the letters in the word *resolution*. Your words should be three letters long or longer.

(Possible answers include rest, solution, tool(s), tile(s), rise, Nile, note, tone, unit, soil, sole, store, and stolen.)

December 31

How much time per day do you spend in a car or a bus? We will figure out a total for the class, and then convert that total to days, weeks, months, and perhaps even years.

January 2

How much time per week do you spend in activities such as Scout meetings, music lessons, or team sports activities? Survey your classmates' answers to this question, then make a graph showing the outcome of your survey.

December 30

The plastic rings that hold six-packs of cans together have been causing trouble for wildlife. Describe uses you can think of for these rings. For example, a person could attach many of them together to make a volleyball net.

January 3

You live in an area of the country where it hardly ever snows. Suddenly, there is a big snowstorm during the night. When you wake your parent(s) to tell them that your school has announced a snow holiday, they have doubts about your story. Describe three methods you can use to convince them that your story is true.

December 29

I will perform some math magic. I want everyone to write down a number. Double it. Add 5. Add 12. Subtract 3. Divide by 2. Subtract your original number. When I say so, I want everyone to say his or her answer aloud.

(Everyone's answer will be 7.)

January 4

How many square hamburgers would it take to cover your classroom floor? Assume that the hamburgers are three inches by three inches. Use paper and pencil for drawing or figuring if it helps you.

December 28

I will list three letters. List all the words that you can think of that contain those letters in order. Score 1 point for each word that begins with those letters. Score 3 points for words in which those letters appear at the beginning or the end. The letters are *w*, *a*, and *l*.

January 5

The weather is so bad that only six students out of your entire class show up for school. You are allowed to play games *all* day. Plan a schedule for your game day.

December 27

A certain clock has three hands: an hour hand, a minute hand, and a second hand. When one hand is on the 7, one hand is on the 12, and one hand is on the 5, what times could it be?

(It could be 5:00, 7:00, 5:35, 7:25, 12:25, or 12:35.)

January 6

Design a picture that is made up entirely of circles. Vary the sizes of the circles and try to arrange them in an original way.

December 26

This time of year is snowy in many parts of the country. Name ten things you can do in snow that you cannot do during warm weather.

(Answers may include snow skiing, tobogganing, sledding, having snowball fights, making snowmen, cross-country skiing, and going on sleigh rides.)

January 7

Have you ever noticed that some words are often seen together in pairs? Some examples are *soup* and *crackers*, *aches* and *pains*, *lost* and *found*, and *ups* and *downs*. Make a list of other common word pairs.

(Answers may include knife *and* fork, hither *and* yon, salt *and* pepper, black *and* blue, ins *and* outs, *etc.)*

December 25

You are wrapping a present at the last minute. You find that your package is too large for the wrapping paper you have. You don't have time to go to the store. What can you do?

(Possible answers include wrapping the present in a comic page, shelf paper, decorated plastic bags, or a trash bag. You could also decorate the box itself.)

January 8

Many deaf people know sign language. This language includes a hand sign for each letter of the alphabet. Create your own hand alphabet. Try to make the signs resemble the actual letters so that your signs are easy to remember.

December 24

You are going to visit relatives during the holidays. Your car gets 20 miles per gallon, and the trip is 800 miles one way. If gas costs $1.05 per gallon, how much will gas cost for the trip there and back? How long will the journey to your relatives' home take if you travel 60 m.p.h. and stops total 1 hour?

(Gas will cost $84.00. The trip will take about 14 1/2 hours.)

January 9

Sally accidentally dropped her boot into quicksand. The boot is 14 inches tall and is sinking at a rate of 1/4 inch each minute. How long will it take for the book to completely disappear? *(56 minutes)* If you were Sally, would you throw in the other boot too, or would you keep a single unmatched boot?

December 23

You oversleep on the morning you are to pick up your lottery winnings. If you do not get there in time, the committee will award the money to someone else. Suddenly, you realize that someone has stolen all your clothing. What will you do? List many possible solutions.

January 10

Use two pieces of notebook paper or less to create the characters for a puppet play. Be prepared to present the play for your classmates.

December 22

A truck driver sees a sign warning of a low bridge but it is too late. His truck becomes wedged under the bridge. He cannot move forward or backward. A tow truck comes, but it is unable to loosen the truck. What can be done to solve this problem?

(Air can be let out of the tires to lower the truck.)

January 11

How is a snowball like a pea? List as many similarities as you can.

(Answers may include the facts that both are round, both are natural, and both are sometimes frozen.)

December 21

Your mother gave you $10.00 to purchase food for dinner. When you checked out at the grocery store, the total came to $11.32. What can you do to solve this problem?

January 12

It is the year 3000 A.D. Nothing is left of the 1990's except for exhibits in the Smells Museum. What odors do you think should be in the 1990's exhibit? List at least twenty odors.

December 20

You have just received a package full of dishes. There are 90 dishes in the package. Half of them are broken. Two out of every five of the remaining dishes are cracked. How many dishes are in good condition?

(Twenty-seven dishes are in good condition.)

January 13

What would happen if all horses had wings like the mythological creature Pegasus? List as many possibilities as you can.

December 19

Create a definition for the word *success*. Then name three people that you think are successful and write why you consider them successful.

January 14

Write a division word problem about your favorite food. Trade papers with a classmate and work his or her problem. When both of you have finished, trade back so that you can check the answer to the problem that you wrote.

December 18

Your new puppy is very mischievous. Suddenly he has grown wings. What new problems might that cause?

January 15

It's creative storytelling time. I'll give you twelve words, and you make up a story that includes those words. Who will be the first volunteer? The words are *twins, bleachers, football, actor, plane, ink, triangle, crocodile, toupee, German, telephone,* and *acrobat.*

December 17

You were supposed to make a pine cone bird feeder for your aunt as a gift. You've lost the directions, so you decide to make up your own directions. Write your directions clearly so that someone else could follow them.

January 16

Draw floor plans for your dream house. Make them as detailed as you can. Then write a paragraph describing your house.

December 16

List as many uses as you can for an empty egg carton.

(Possible answers include using it as a paint tray, an ice tray, a storage tray, or as a material for arts and crafts.)

January 17

What are all the numbers between one and fifty that can be divided evenly by two all the way down to a quotient of one? Sixteen will work. $16 \div 2 = 8 \div 2 = 4 \div 2 = 2 \div 2 = 1$ Twenty-six, however, will not work. $26 \div 2 = 13 \div 2 = 6\ 1/2$ If you get a fraction in the quotient, the number does not work.

(The numbers are 2, 4, 8, 16, and 32.)

December 15

Coco Chanel was a French fashion designer. She once said, "There are people who have money and people who are rich." Explain this quotation in your own words.

January 18

On a frigid day in January, a boy comes home from school to find water dripping from the ceiling. How many possible explanations can you list?

December 14

Many dinosaurs were herbivores. These are animals that eat mostly plants. Name other animals that you know of that are herbivores.

January 19

A friend has walked out onto a frozen lake. The ice is thin and is beginning to crack. Your friend is calling out for help. What can you do to help your friend without endangering yourself?

December 13

List all of the occupations you can think of that begin with the letter *r*.

(Answers may include radiologist, rabbi, referee, and repair person.)

January 20

A palindrome is a number that reads the same forward and backward, such as 121121. By adding a number and its reverse, and doing the same to the sum of those numbers, you eventually reach a palindrome. For example, 12 + 12 = 33 and 39 + 93 = 132 + 231 = 363. What palindromes do you get when you start with 59, 69, and 79?

(59 = 1111, 69 = 4884, and 79 = 44044)

December 12

List all the triangles you can see in this room. Now
list the circles you see.

January 21

Use at least five book titles to design a crossword puzzle. Vary your clues and make them challenging. Be sure that you know how to spell the titles correctly so that you create the correct number of spaces in your puzzle.

December 11

Make a list of gifts you could make and give as gifts to relatives and friends. Try to make the materials as inexpensive as possible. Be creative!

January 22

Imagine that the landfills are all filled and there is no longer any trash pick up. What can you and your neighbors do to take care of the garbage problem?

December 10

Use the names of at least seven sports to create a crossword puzzle. Be sure your words are spelled correctly, and make your clues challenging.

January 23

Make a list of all the ways that you could slide down a snow-covered hill. Be creative!

(Answers may include various equipment to use and/or various positions one could take while sliding.)

December 9

A girl in your class used to make fun of everyone. Lately, she is very quiet and never pokes fun at anyone. What reasons can you think of for her behavior?

January 24

Using only one piece of construction paper, create the best Native American village possible in ____ minutes.

December 8

A stack of eight pennies is about 1/2 inch high. How many pennies would be required to build a stack as tall as you? How many pennies do you think you could actually stack before the stack would fall over?

January 25

Do you believe in extraterrestrial beings, otherwise known as aliens? Why might their existence be considered a positive thing? Why might it be considered negative?

December 7

How is a flea like a kangaroo? List as many similarities as possible.

(Answers may include the facts that both are alive, both hop, and both eat.)

January 26

A school lunch costs 85¢. You enjoy cafeteria food and buy your lunch every day. You bring a crisp dollar bill each day and receive the proper amount of change which you deposit in a piggy bank hidden in your desk. At the end of the school year, how much money do you have in that bank? Assume there are 180 school days in the year.
(The answer is $27.00.)

December 6

It makes everyone feel wonderful to get a note saying something nice. Write a positive note to three people in the classroom. You must sign your name on the notes.

January 27

An American statesman named Cordell Hull was quoted as saying, "Never insult an alligator until after you have crossed the river." What do you think he meant by this quote?

December 5

If you were to give awards to animals, which animal would win the medal for being the most loyal? Which animal would win the medal for being most active? Which animal would win the medal for having the roughest skin? Create three other categories and tell which animals would win those awards.

January 28

List as many uses as you possibly can for a paper clip.

(Possible answers include using a paper clip as a fishhook, an ornament hanger, or a screwdriver.)

December 4

Design a classroom in which every student could
see the teacher and the chalkboard equally. Your
plan can be as imaginative as you like.

January 29

How many legs are there in this classroom? Don't leave anyone or anything out. Count desks, tables, people, and any objects that would qualify as having legs. We will see how many of you get the same total.

December 3

A sequential date is one whose numbers go in ascending order (3/4/56) or descending order (9/8/76). What is the next ascending sequential date after 6/7/89? *(1/2/34)* What is the next ascending sequential date after that? *(2/3/45)* What are some other sequential dates?

(Other dates include 4/5/67, 5/6/78, 8/7/65, 7/6/54, 6/5/43, 5/4/32, and 4/3/21.)

January 30

Imagine that you and a friend have a piece of string and a table tennis ball. Invent as many games as you can using only these two items.

December 2

In honor of the first snowfall of the year, you are going to serve a dinner with all white foods. List every white food you can think of and then write out your menu. Remember to select a variety of foods.

January 31

You and a friend have discovered an abandoned town. Now it is yours. What will you name the town? How will you encourage people to live there? What rules will the citizens of your town have to follow?

December 1

How many stacked hamburgers would it take to go from pole to pole through the center of the earth? The distance is about 7,900 miles. Imagine that each hamburger is 2 inches thick. How many burgers will equal a foot? *(6)* Remember that there are 5,280 feet in a mile.

(It would take 250,272,000 hamburgers.)

February 1

Let's do a mental math problem. Begin with the number that is 5 more than 7. Increase this number by 8, twice. Add 20. Now reduce the answer by half. What is the number?

(The answer is twenty-four.)

November 30

Place the symbols +, −, x, or ÷ between the numbers to make these equations true:

1.) 2 2 2 2 = 10
2.) 8 7 3 2 = 7
3.) 10 3 3 7 = 3
4.) 8 2 9 9 = 4

(1. x, x, +   2. +, +, +   3. −, x, ÷   4. ÷, x, ÷)

February 2

How is a fingerprint like a snowflake? List as many ways as you possibly can.

(Answers may include the facts that individual snowflakes or fingerprints are unlike any others, both are small, and both can be wiped away.)

November 29

Here's a mental math problem for you. Begin with the smallest two-digit number you can think of. Double that number. Now subtract 8. Add 10. Double the number. What is the answer?

(The answer is 44.)

February 3

If you could meet any United States president, living or dead, who would it be and what would you talk about?

November 28

You need 200 ice cubes for a party that starts in 8 hours. Your ice cube trays hold ten cubes each, and it takes 4 hours for the cubes to freeze. What is the least number of ice cube trays that you will need to make the ice cubes for the party?

(If you empty the trays and refill them in four hours, you will need ten ice cube trays.)

February 4

A new pencil that has not been sharpened is nearly seven inches long. How many new pencils placed end to end would be needed to make a single line around the perimeter of this classroom?

(Answers will depend on the size of the classroom.)

November 27

Your younger sister comes to you with a ring stuck on her finger. You pull and pull but it will not come off. What can you do to solve this problem?

(Possible solutions include using soap and water or oil to make her hand slippery so that the ring will slip off.)

February 5

You have a pet grindantua (nonsense word).
What does it look like? What would you feed it?
Where did you get it?

November 26

Jessica is five years old and her sister is four times as old. How many times older will her sister be in ten more years?

(In ten years Jessica's sister will be twice as old as Jessica is.)

February 6

What would happen if we could grow new limbs like a lizard grows a new tail? List as many possibilities as you can.

November 25

Anagrams are formed by rearranging the letters in a word. Find at least two anagrams for each of these words: *thus, nips, ores, snug,* and *tabs.*

(huts, shut; spin, snip, pins; sore, rose; guns, sung; stab, bats)

February 7

The year 1991 is the only palindrome year during the twentieth century. A palindrome reads the same backwards and forwards. What was the palindrome year during the 1600's? *(1661)* The 1700's? *(1771)* The 1800's? *(1881)* What will the palindrome year be between the year 2000 and the year 2100? *(2002)*

November 24

Write a five-letter word for a strong carton. The letters in this word can be rearranged to spell three other words. What are they?

(The letters in the word crate *can be rearranged to spell* react, cater, *and* trace.)

February 8

Write a multiplication word problem about a hobby. We will trade papers and work the problems. Then we will trade back and correct them. Be sure you have figured out the correct answer before you give your problem to anyone.

November 23

A man is at the grocery store. He buys 2 1/2 pounds of meat at $1.50 a pound, 2 dozen oranges at $.79 a dozen, 9 avacados at 3 for $1.00, 1 pound of cheese at $3.52 a pound, and 3 pounds of grapes at $1.29 a pound. How much change should he get back from his $20 bill?

(He should get $4.28 as change.)

February 9

It's creative storytelling time. I will give you twelve words and as a group you will create a story that includes all twelve words. Who would like to begin the story? The words are *stars, homework, polo, liquid, sleet, sand, rainbow, circus, diamond, cell, bale,* and *cheap.*

November 22

What word rhymes with a word that means close by, has a homophone that names an animal that lives in the woods, and has an anagram (scrambled letters) that means to get meaning from letters and words.

(**Dear**—*near, deer, read.*)

February 10

You and your family are going on vacation. Your suitcase is the only one missing at the end of your flight. Create as many explanations as you can for this situation.

November 21

Write the word *Thanksgiving*. Divide this into two words and delete the first word. Switch the fourth and sixth letters. Change the first letter to a *p*. Change the third letter to *l* and the fifth letter to *r*. Add a letter to spell the name for one of the people who took part in the first Thanksgiving.

(The word is pilgrim.*)*

February 11

Franz caught thirty butterflies and placed them in a special box made of cloth. His brother came along and made a small hole in the box. One butterfly escaped every forty-five minutes. How long would it take before all the butterflies were gone?

(It would take 22.5 hours.)

November 20

I am thinking of a number. It is less than 25. It is not an even number. It is divisible by two numbers less than 7 excluding one. What is the number?

(The number is 15.)

February 12

Valentines Day is coming. Draw a complicated picture made up entirely of hearts of varying sizes.

November 19

Rearrange the digits in your phone number to create the largest number possible. Now rearrange them into the smallest number possible. Subtract the smaller 7-digit number from the larger one. Determine who in the class has the largest difference between these two numbers.

February 13

Make a list of the sweetest things you could possibly do for a parent, a brother or sister, a teacher, or a friend.

November 18

List as many uses as you possibly can for a handkerchief.

(Possible answers include using a handkerchief as a rag, a flag, a rope, a scarf, a patch, or a bag.)

February 14

In honor of Valentine's Day, you are going to serve a dinner made up of red foods. List every red food you can think of and then write out your menu. Remember to select a variety of foods.

November 17

"A man must take the fat with the lean." How would you explain this quote by Charles Dickens?

February 15

Use at least five last names of United States presidents to design a crossword puzzle. Try to make your clues challenging. Be sure to watch your spelling!

November 16

How many ways are there to say "thank-you"? List as many verbal and nonverbal ways as possible.

(Possible answers include notes, cards, phone calls, telegrams, hugs, and handshakes.)

February 16

You have just come home from school and you find that your dog, Buster, has eaten eleven chocolate candy bars. No one is home. You have read that chocolate can be toxic to dogs. What should you do?

November 15

How would you feel if all the schools were closed down and children were taught by computers in their homes? What things would change? Would your education be better or worse?

February 17

List all of the American foods that you can. Now list all the foods that you know come from other countries. Compare your list with your classmates' lists.

November 14

There are hundreds of alphabet books in bookstores. You have been asked to create a new and different type of alphabet book that children will love. Write and illustrate your new book.

February 18

Make as many new words as you can from the letters in the word *relationship*. Make your words three letters long or longer.

(Answers include relation, ship, shirt, late, rate, tip, hip, sip, snip, slip, tail, tale, tailor, ration, torn, snare, *and* snore.)

November 13

Billy was going to make cookies for everyone in his club. His recipe called for 2 1/4 cups of flour and 3/4 cup butter and would make enough cookies for 6 children. There were 18 children in the club. How much flour and butter would Billy need to feed all of the club members?

(He would need 6 3/4 cups of flour and 2 1/4 cups of butter.)

February 19

Using only three pieces of newspaper and some masking tape, construct the highest tower you can in ___ minutes. (This activity works very well in groups!)

November 12

I am thinking of a number. It is a palindrome number. That means it reads the same backwards and forwards. It has four digits. The first digit is greater than 5. If you add the digits together, they equal 12. What is the number?

(The number is 6006.)

February 20

List as many uses as you can for a saucepan.

(Possible answers include a drinking cup, a hat, and a paddle.)

November 11

How is oatmeal like a sweater? List as many similarities as you possibly can.

(Possible answers include the facts that both are often used in cool weather, both are used by people, and both can help warm a person.)

February 21

Give each letter of the alphabet a numerical code such as A=10, B=15, C=20. (In this case, the word *cab* would be written 20, 10, 15.) Write a note in code and let another student try to decipher it.

November 10

You have been asked to design a rug that encourages people to move to a certain part of a room. Think about what might make people want to go to a certain area, and design your rug on a piece of paper.

(Possible answers include designing a rug with arrows that point toward a certain area, or using warm colors in one area and harsh colors in all others.)

February 22

Abraham Lincoln said, "No man is good enough to govern another man without the other's consent." What did Lincoln mean by this quote?

November 9

Answer these multiplication problems. See if you can determine a pattern for the answers. 7 x 99, 8 x 99, 3 x 99, 5 x 99.

(693, 792, 297, 495; You can find the answer by subtracting the first factor from that number times 100. For example, 7 x 99 = 7 less than 700.)

February 23

If you could fly like a bird, what would you do with your flying skill? What kind of job would you seek?

November 8

Create plans for a dream tree house. Make it as perfect as you can. Money is no object. What features will it have? Where will it be?

February 24

Using only circles and rectangles, draw a house in the woods. Include as much detail as you can.

November 7

A local television station has offered a reward to anyone who can hide in his or her home for three hours without being found by family members. List all the possible places you could hide.

February 25

Add operation symbols (+, −, x, or ÷) to the following equations to make them true:

1.	4	2	4	2	=	6
2.	4	6	6	4	=	1
3.	8	8	8	8	=	8
4.	5	4	3	2	=	8

(1. x, +, ÷   2. +, −, +   3. −, x, +   4. +, −, +)

November 6

List all of the occupations you can think of that start with the letter *d*.

(Possible answers include dentist, doctor, designer, dietitian, dancer, director, dean, delivery person, and driver.)

February 26

Let's challenge your brain with a little mental math. Take today's date (*26*) and subtract 11. Now take what's left and multiply it by 2. Divide by 10. Hold up your fingers to show the answer.

(The answer is 3.)

November 5

January 1, 1911, 1/1/11 was an interesting date. All the numbers in this date were the same. What was the most recent date with all the numbers alike? *(8/8/88)* What will the next two dates like this be? *(9/9/99 and 1/1/11)*

February 27

John brought twenty-six cupcakes for a class treat, but a new student enrolled making twenty-seven class members. How should the treats be distributed?

November 4

Sometimes when you are baby-sitting your little sister, your mother asks you to walk to the grocery store. The whole time you are in the store, your sister screams for candy. What are five ways you can handle this problem?

February 28

Figure out the name of a fruit whose letters can be rearranged to create a word that means inexpensive.

(The letters in the word peach *can be rearranged to spell* cheap.*)*

November 3

How many stacked-up pizzas would it take to reach from Earth to the Moon? Let's suppose that each pizza is two inches high. How many pizzas would it take to make a foot? *(6)* Remember that there are 5,280 feet in a mile. The distance to the moon is about 239,000 miles.

(It would take 7,571,520,000 pizzas.)

February 29

February 29th occurs only once every four years, during a leap year. How many leap years occur during a decade? Think carefully. This question may not be as easy as you think.

(There could be two or three leap years during a decade. There would be three if the first or second year in the decade were a leap year. Otherwise, there would be only two.)

November 2

You wake up and find that you have been asleep for five years. What are the first things you will ask about? What will you want to do or see first?

March 1

You are required to read fifty books by May 16. It is March 1 and you have read twenty-eight books. How many books per week will you have to read in order to fulfill your requirement?

(50 – 28 = 22 books to read. There are 77 days (11 weeks) between March 1 and May 16. 22 ÷ 11 = 2 books per week)

November 1

Do you have a pet? Do your classmates have pets? Make a graph showing what types of pets, if any, your classmates have.

March 2

After spending two years on a treasure-finding trip, your group comes across a huge metal chest full of treasure. List all the things you find when the chest is opened.

October 31

While walking in the mall, you overhear three teen-age boys planning to mug little children on Halloween night. Your little brother had all his candy stolen by older kids last year. What are three things you could do?

March 3

If you were to give awards to animals, which of them would receive the following awards: Fastest Animal, Slowest Animal, Most Intelligent Animal, Least Intelligent Animal, Ugliest Animal, Most Beautiful Animal, Fiercest Animal, and Most Lovable Animal.

October 30

You have just bought a pumpkin that you are going to make into a jack-o'-lantern for Halloween. When you get home, you find that the pumpkin cracked during the ride. How can you still make use of the pumpkin?

(Possible answers include using it to make pumpkin pie, cooking the seeds, saving and planting the seeds, or working the crack into part of your jack-o'-lantern design.)

March 4

You have been asked to draw faces for the Portrait Gallery of Emotions. Draw the appropriate facial expressions for the following emotions: fear, happiness, sadness, anger, disappointment, confusion, elation, surprise, and exhaustion.

October 29

You are having a Halloween party. You want to give a small pumpkin to each of eleven guests. Store A is running a special that when you buy three small pumpkins for $2.00, you get a fourth one free. Store B is selling small pumpkins for $.55 each. Which store offers a better deal?

(At Store A you can get 12 pumpkins for $6.00 and at Store B you would pay $6.05 for eleven pumpkins.)

March 5

Penny's polo pony is fifteen hands high. A "hand" is four inches. How tall is the pony? (*60 inches*) How many hands high would you be? (*Height in inches divided by 4.*) How do you think people came up with that method of measuring horses?

October 28

Anagrams are words that are created by rearranging the letters in another word. Find at least two anagrams for each of these words: *traps, break, pears, steal,* and *peals.*

(strap, parts; brake, baker; pares, reaps, spare, spear; stale, slate, steal; leaps, pales)

March 6

Using two pieces of notebook paper or less, create a new game for two or more people to play.

October 27

Make as many words as you can out of the letters in the word *Halloween*. Make your words three letters long or longer.

(Possible answers include hall, wall, wheel, heel, lane, whale, all, low, new, how, *and* now.)

March 7

How is a cat like a hot water bottle? List as many similarities as you possibly can.

(Answers may include the facts that both contain a warm liquid, both can keep you warm, and both can be comforting.)

October 26

List as many uses as you possibly can for a sponge.

(Possible answers include using a sponge as a washcloth, a paintbrush, or a pillow.)

March 8

A can of soup contains approximately 11 ounces and will serve three people when mixed with an equal amount of water. How many cans of soup would be needed to serve everyone in your class one serving? How many cans would you need to serve all the students in your school one serving?

(Divide number of students in class and number of students in school by three.)

October 25

Ben Franklin once said, "Don't throw stones at your neighbors' (windows) if your own windows are glass." What do you think he meant by this?

March 9

What might happen if there were no drivers' licenses? List as many possibilities as you can.

October 24

You have just been informed that your entire family is moving to Spain. What are your feelings? What must you do to prepare for the move?

March 10

When you move into your new home and walk out into the backyard, you are surprised to see little bare spots all over the lawn. How many explanations can you list to explain this?

October 23

Make as many new words as you can out of the letters in the word *advertising*. Create words three letters long or longer.

(Possible answers include *vent, sing, sting, dig, stir, trade, strange, singe, grin, dear, read,* and *grin*.)

March 11

Abby's mother stopped her from throwing away a paper grocery bag. She said it would be easy to recycle. How many uses can you come up with for the grocery bag?

October 22

Ribster's Dictionary of American Slang has asked you to write down the present slang words being used in your school and neighborhood. Make a glossary of the slang words you hear and use. Include the meaning of each word.

March 12

Use the names of at least five occupations to design a crossword puzzle. Try to make your clues challenging. Watch your spelling!

October 21

Use the names of at least five countries to create a crossword puzzle. Be sure you spell the names correctly and create challenging clues.

March 13

You have a choice between a comforter set with matching pillows for $100 or one for $120 with 20% off. Which is the better deal?

(The one that is 20% off of $120 is a better deal. It costs $96.)

October 20

It takes 53 beads to string a necklace. Grace has 1,000 beads. How many necklaces can she string? *(18)* Will she have any beads left over? *(Yes, 46)*

March 14

Make a list of all the headlines that you would love to see in a newspaper.

October 19

An old man gets on a bus and speaks to the driver in a whisper. Then he immediately gets off the bus. Think of three explanations for the man's behavior.

March 15

Bill had 557 baseball cards. A dealer offered him ten cents for every card except for 15 cards which were worth $3 each, 5 cards worth $10 each, and one card worth $45. How much was Bill offered for the entire collection?

*(557 − 21 = 536 cards   536 x .10 = $53.60   15 x 3 = $45
5 x 10 = $50 $53.60 + $45 + $50 + $45 = $193.60)*

October 18

How many people in the room have blue eyes?
How many have brown eyes? How many have
green eyes? Make a graph to show the results of
your survey.

March 16

If an alien offered you a ride in a spaceship, would you go? Why or why not? Where do you think the alien might take you?

October 17

Draw a detailed treasure map of the classroom. Write directions from the classroom door to a "treasure." Describe the incredible treasure that the finder will receive. Fold up your paper and turn it in. After I look at the maps, we will take turns following some of them to find the "treasures."

March 17

In honor of St. Patrick's Day, your class created 220 shamrock pins. It cost 4¢ to make each pin. You sold 177 of them for 50¢ each. You sold the remaining pins on March 18 for 20¢ each. How much money did your class make on this project? Remember to subtract your costs.

*(220 x .04 = $8.80   177 x .5 = $88.50   220 – 177 = 43
43 x .20 =$8.60 $88.50 + $8.60 – $8.80 = $88.30)*

October 16

Imagine this scene. Your best friend is handing you $100 and you are not happy. Think of as many explanations as possible for this scene.

March 18

Mark Twain said, "A man cannot be comfortable without his own approval." What do you believe he meant by this?

October 15

You just bought a new horse. It will need shoes every six weeks throughout the year. The shoe man charges $35.00 for his services each time. How much will you pay for shoeing in a year's time?

(The answer is $280.00.)

March 19

List as many uses as you possibly can for a shoelace.

(Possible answers include using it as a cat toy, a bracelet, a tie, a hair ribbon, book binding, or as a small clothesline.)

October 14

It's creative storytelling time. I'll give you ten words to use in a story. Who would like to begin the story? The words are *snowballs*, *Florida*, *cushions*, *garbage*, *limousine*, *soldier*, *stapler*, *cowboy*, *butter*, and *sign*.

March 20

Here is a mental math problem for you. Begin with the largest possible two-digit number. Subtract 10. Reduce that number by 39. Divide the answer in half. What is the answer?

(The answer is 25.)

October 13

How is a pair of scissors like a pair of eye glasses? List as many similarities as you can.

(Possible answers include the facts that both are for human use, both have two rounded parts, and both are often made of similar material.)

March 21

In honor of spring, you are going to serve a dinner made up entirely of green foods. List every green food you can think of and then write out your menu. Remember to select a variety of foods.

October 12

Betty wanted a book on fossils which was marked
$15.95. She had $16.00 but she could not afford
the book. Do you know why?

(Tax is added to the price of a book.)

March 22

You have been offered $1,000 to carry a giant peanut everywhere you go for a week. You are not allowed to mention the cash offer to anyone, and the peanut is the size of a large cat. Will you carry it? If so, how will you carry it? How will you explain why you are carrying the peanut?

October 11

Imagine that the driving age were lowered to your age. What would be the best thing about this change? What would be the worst thing? Would you want to learn to drive right away?

March 23

Listen carefully. Sal bought 627 horses. He bought 80 Arabians, 500 thoroughbreds, and 47 Lippizans. How many horses did he buy?

(Students should not need to do any figuring. The answer was provided in the first sentence of the problem.)

October 10

See if you can subtract these numbers in your head. 47–16 equals what? *(31)* 645–33 equals what? *(612)* 4239–138 equals what? *(4101)* 8000–1 equals what? *(7999)* 8000–50 equals what? *(7950)*

March 24

A ball, a boat, a bear, and a pail each belong to one of four children, Tommy, John, Cathy, and Terry. Tommy's toy cannot hold anything. Cathy's toy is smooth and rolls. John has a fun place to play with his toy when he borrows Terry's toy. Which toy belongs to which child?

(Tommy–bear, John–boat, Cathy–ball, Terry–pail)

October 9

Many schools require that students wear uniforms. Design a school uniform that would be comfortable as well as good looking.

March 25

Susan and Linda play tennis each week. They average 15 games each week. If Susan usually wins 2/3 of the games, how many games will she win in 4 weeks? *(40 games)* In 12 weeks? *(120 games)* In 6 months? *(240 games)*

October 8

Have you ever heard the expression "a cat has nine lives"? What do you think it means? What changes would occur if humans had nine lives? List many possibilities.

March 26

You are traveling on a highway in a car with a friend. The car breaks down and will not move. You are halfway between Exit A and Exit B. What will you do?

October 7

Each year, a school holds a contest to see who can design a container that will protect an egg when it is dropped from a high tower. What materials would you use to create such a container?

March 27

Write the name of a tool used to chop wood. Then substitute one letter in that word and rearrange the letters to spell a word that describes what teeth often do when a person is very cold.

(A hatchet is used to chop wood, and teeth chatter.)

October 6

What is the average number of letters in the first names of the students in this class? What method could you use to determine this answer?

March 28

If you had stuck to a New Year's resolution to eat one orange every day, how many oranges would you have eaten after finishing today's orange? If each of those oranges had twelve sections, how many orange sections would you have eaten as of today?

(31 + 28 + 28 = 87 oranges (88 oranges if it is a leap year), 87 x 12 = 1044 sections (1056 sections if it is a leap year))

October 5

A girl's grandmother is only five years older than the girl's mother. How do you explain that?

(The grandmother is her father's mother, and the girl's father is much younger than her mother.)

March 29

Which salary is highest: $196 per week, $852 per
month, or $10,608 per year?

*($196 per week equals $10,192 per year. $852 per month
equals $10,224 per year. $10,608 per year is highest.)*

October 4

Design a picture made only of triangles. Be creative!

March 30

A salesman checked the odometer on his car at the beginning of his trip. It read 29,844 miles. At the end of his trip, it read 31,117. If his company pays him 24¢ a mile for gas, how much money does the company owe him?

(31,117 − 29,844 = 1273 miles   1273 x .24 = $305.52)

October 3

How many hamburgers would it take to go around the world at the equator? Let's assume that a hamburger is 4 inches wide. How many burgers will equal a foot? (3) Remember there are 5,280 feet in a mile. The equatorial circumference of the earth is about 24,902 miles.

(3 x 5280 x 24,902 = 394.447.680 hamburgers)

March 31

You have decided to plan a surprise party for your best friend. Make a list of the decisions you will have to make about the party.

(Answers should include decisions about time, place, menu, invitations, entertainment, seating, cost, and more.)

October 2

Use only one piece of paper to create the best bowl possible in ___ minutes. Think about the characteristics of a bowl that are important.

April 1

A close relative who was scheduled to entertain children in a local hospital is too ill to perform. You will have to go instead. Describe three things that you could do to entertain the children.

October 1

Your mother plugged up a hole in the roof because she saw a bat fly out of it. You walk into your room and find bats hanging from every lamp, picture, door frame, and piece of furniture. What will you do to get rid of the bats?

April 2

Using only two pieces of notebook paper, construct the best model of a farm possible in _____ minutes.

September 30

What word rhymes with the word for a royal person, has a homonym that means to twist and squeeze, and has an anagram that is the word for a happy smile?

(ring—king, wring, grin)

April 3

What would the world be like if no one could speak? What would it be like if no one could hear? What would the world be like if no one could see? What would the world be like if people could not do any of these things?

September 29

Anagrams are words that can be made by scrambling the letters of another word. Write two or more anagrams for each of these words: *vile, stop, pets, stone,* and *slain.*

(evil, veil, live; pots, tops; pest, step; notes, onset, tones; nails, snail)

April 4

"Truth stood on one side and ease on the other; it has often been so." This is a quotation by Theodore Parker, a famous clergyman and abolitionist. Write what you believe Parker meant by this quotation.

September 28

I'm thinking of a number. It is greater than 10. It is divisible by 4. It is less than 25. It does not have a 2 in it. What is the number?

(The number is 16.)

April 5

List as many uses as you possibly can for a thimble.

(Answers may include using a thimble as a tiny cup, a stopper, a measuring device, or as a game piece.)

September 27

Get ready for a mental math problem! Start with the number 2. Now double it. Multiply that number by 5. Divide the answer in half. Add 4. Subtract 3. What is the answer?

(The answer is 11.)

April 6

Jalena was gift-wrapping a red and yellow beach ball. She had spent fifteen minutes inflating the ball. As she put it into the fancy box that she had bought, she realized the ball was too large for the box. Jalena had no other boxes and it was time to leave for the party. What are some possible solutions to this problem?

(The easiest solution would be to let air out of the ball.)

September 26

Fold a piece of paper several times at different angles. Write a message on a surface of the paper that is made up of many different parts of the paper. Unfold the paper, crumple it a bit to disguise your original folds, and give it to another student to be decoded.

April 7

You find a great $150 C.D. player on sale at 25% off. How much will it cost? (*$112.50*) Create another problem that involves a discount.

September 25

If you could turn into an animal, which animal would you be? Why? What would you do as that animal?

April 8

Design and draw a machine that helps people in some way.

September 24

Using only one piece of paper, construct the best child's toy possible in ___ minutes.

April 9

Try to solve these problems in your head as I say them. It helps to picture them in your mind. 2000 + 3000 + 500 equals what? *(5500)* Try again! 8000 + 8000 − 2000 − 1 equals what? *(13999)* One more! 500 + 3000 + 500 equals what? *(4000)*

September 23

Make as many words as you can out of the word *brachiosaurus*. The words should be three letters long or longer.

(Possible answers include roar, soar, crab, Russia, car, rib, crass, brass, hiss, hair, *and* orb.)

April 10

How many hours of sleep do you think you've had during your lifetime? Keep in mind that babies spend a great deal of time sleeping. Perhaps some of you still do. Now figure out how many hours of sleep you expect to have during your entire lifetime.

September 22

Make a list of ten people that you would like to know personally. Now put your list in order so that the first person on the list is the person you'd like to meet most, and so on.

April 11

What would happen if everyone moved away from rural areas?

(Answers may include overpopulation in cities and food shortages caused by a lack of farmers.)

September 21

Use the names of at least seven classmates to create a crossword puzzle. Make your clues creative, challenging, and positive. Watch your spelling!

April 12

How is a necklace like a tattoo? List as many similarities as possible.

(Possible answers include the facts that both are ornamental and can be put on by someone else.)

September 20

A man who used to be the sloppiest dresser in the world is now always well dressed. Write down as many explanations as you can for this change.

April 13

Guess the sum of the numbers from 11 through 20? Is it more than 50? Is it more than 100? Is it more than 200? Now figure out the sum to see how close your estimate was.

(The sum is 155.)

September 19

Design the perfect school bus for field trips. Make sure it has everything you need for comfort and entertainment while on the road.

April 14

It's creative storytelling time. I will give you twelve words and as a group you will make up a story that includes those words. Who would like to begin the story? The words are *mansion*, *tonsillectomy*, *tomato*, *dominoes*, *knife*, *spaghetti*, *minister*, *mash*, *spy*, *children*, *berries*, and *cows*.

September 18

How many people in the room are wearing shoes that tie? How many people are wearing slip-ons? How many are wearing another type of shoe? Create a pie graph or a bar graph to show the results of this survey.

April 15

Try to figure out the next number in this pattern:
5, 10, 20, ___. (*40–double the previous number*)
Try this one 1, 2, 4, 7, 11, ___. (*16–add a number
that is greater by one each time*)

September 17

It's your turn to write a math problem. Using four operations one time each (one addition, one subtraction, one multiplication, and one division operation), write a math problem that results in your room number, the school's street address, or today's date.

April 16

Write a description of your favorite animal, but do not name the animal. Describe it in such a way that someone hearing the description could draw the animal and determine what it is. For example, you might say, "This animal walks on four legs." Then a listener would draw four legs. When everyone is ready, I will read some descriptions, and we will see who draws the correct animal.

September 16

You have just been told by a very reliable source that each child in your class will receive $1,000 dollars if every student agrees not to watch television for a month. How will you proceed to make this happen? The donor does have a way to find out if anyone cheats.

April 17

A man who has been known as a penny pincher all his life has suddenly begun handing out money to everyone he meets on the street. Write as many explanations as possible for his behavior.

September 15

Design and decorate a special bookmark which will encourage young children to read. List all your ideas before choosing one for the final product. Be prepared to explain how your bookmark will make reading inviting to children.

April 18

For most people, the length from fingertip to fingertip with outstretched arms is equal to his or her height. Is this true for you? Is it true of people younger or older than you? Find out.

September 14

Multiply 895 x 8 x 0. What did you get? Now multiply that answer by 298. What did you get?

(Emphasize the fact that anything times zero equals zero.)

April 19

There is a scratching sound coming from inside your fireplace. You look closely, but you cannot see anything. What could it be? What will you do about it?

September 13

Imagine that you could shrink to six inches tall any time you wanted to. What would you do with this special talent? What would be the best thing about having this talent? What would be the worst thing about it?

April 20

Take a quick guess at what the sum of all the numbers from one through ten is. Now add those numbers and see how close you came.

(The sum is 55.)

September 12

Bert is writing a report on time management. He figures it will take him 8 hours to complete. Bert only has 1 hour and 15 minutes each day to work on the report. How many days will it take him to finish it?

(It will take him 6 1/2 days to complete the report.)

April 21

Design a crossword puzzle with the names of at least five foods. Make your clues challenging and watch your spelling.

September 11

How is a magician like a teacher? List as many similarities as possible.

(Possible answers include the facts that both people do their job in front of people and they both demonstrate things.)

April 22

Design a picture that is made up of an equal number of circles, triangles, and squares.

September 10

Design a family crest that depicts things that your family is interested in. For example, your crest might include books if your family likes to read.

April 23

Make a list of headlines that you would hate to see in the newspaper.

September 9

A band director had 4 times as many trumpet players as he had flute players. He had twice as many flute players as he had drummers, and half as many drummers as he had clarinet players. If the director had 3 drummers, how many trumpet players did he have? *(24)* What information in this problem is unnecessary? *(The number of clarinet players is unnecessary.)*

April 24

You are offered $150 to go 24 hours without smiling. What might happen as a result of not smiling? How might your relationships at school be affected? How about at home? What else might happen? Is it worth $150 to do this?

September 8

You plan to live in your tree house for two weeks. There is no electricity, but the weather is mild so the temperature will be comfortable. What would you bring for entertainment? What food would you bring? What other items might you need?

April 25

A case of soft drinks (24 cans) costs $4.80. How much does 1 can cost? *(20¢)* How much does half of a case cost? *($2.40)* How much would 17 cans cost? *($3.40)* How many cans of soda could you buy for $7.80? *(39 cans)*

September 7

Redesign the classroom in any way you'd like. Imagine that you could rearrange windows, chalkboard, furniture, etc. How would you arrange the room? Be ready to explain and defend your design.

April 26

A local shopping center must keep three spaces available for handicapped customers. Some patrons who do not need these spaces are not very considerate and park in these spaces. What could be done to keep this from happening?

September 6

What fraction of the wall is made up of windows? How would we find out? What will you use to measure the wall?

April 27

Think of a word for a mischievous elf. *(imp)* Now think of a synonym for the word *steal*. *(rob)* Write the name of a piece of furniture and subtract the first letter. *(table)* Put all of these letters together to make a word that means *not likely*. *(improbable)*

September 5

List ten ingredients that would be on what you would consider to be the worst sandwich in the world. All of the ingredients should be edible.

April 28

Mr. Kelley's gas station makes bank deposits daily. His station is open six days a week. On Monday he deposited $612.50, on Tuesday $512.50, on Wednesday $520.00, on Thursday $700.00, on Friday $975.00 and on Saturday $875.50. What was his average daily deposit?

(The average daily deposit was $699.25.)

September 4

Which is heavier—a pound of feathers or a pound of eggs? *(Neither. They both weigh a pound.)* Try to make up a trick question of your own.

April 29

You have been given a garden plot that is 8 feet by 4 feet. You plan to divide the land equally between 4 crops. How many square feet are in your garden? On how many square feet will you plant each crop? What crops would you choose to plant?

(The garden is 32 square feet. Each crop would cover 8 square feet of land. Crops planted will vary.)

September 3

Your grandparents have offered to give you one of their horses if you promise to exercise it daily. The stable is only two blocks from your house, but you have to go to piano and chess lessons three nights a week. How can you still exercise the horse each day?

(A possible solution would be to ride the horse to the lessons.)

April 30

I will list three letters. Create a list of words that contain the letters in order. Score 1 point for each word that begins with these letters. Score 3 points for words that have these letters in the middle or at the end. We will see who gets the highest score. The letters are *e, v,* and *e.*

September 2

There are 20 teachers in your school. Each teacher uses an average of 2 sticks of chalk per day. A box of chalk holds 12 sticks. A carton of chalk holds 12 boxes and costs $5.50. If there are 180 days in a school year, how many cartons of chalk does your school need to purchase for the year? How much will the chalk cost?

(They need to purchase 50 cartons. It will cost $275.00.)

May 1

Design personalized stationery for a parent. Put his or her initials or a special drawing at the top of the page. Then design a matching envelope. This would make a good Mother's Day or Father's Day gift.

September 1

Your desk is full of books, but how many pages are there in all of your books combined? Find out who has the most book pages in his or her desk.

May 2

Make a list of all the squares and rectangles that you see in this room.

August 31

The hall where your graduation is being held holds a maximum of 300 people. There are 29 people in your class, and 10 faculty members plan to attend. The remaining seats will be split evenly between the graduates. How many people can you invite to your graduation?

(Each graduate can invite 9 guests.)

May 3

You are in a room that locks with a key from the inside and the outside. You have only a newspaper and a paper clip. The key is in the keyhole on the other side of the door. What can you do to get out?

(Slide most of an open page of newspaper under the door. Then straighten the paper clip and push the key out of the keyhole. Hopefully, the key will fall onto the newspaper. Next, pull the newspaper, with the key on it, back to your side of the door and use the key to open the door.)

August 30

Your friend owes you $10. He tells you that he knows he paid you back because he remembers placing a ten dollar bill between pages 21 and 22 of one of your school books. You are sure that your friend is mistaken. Why?

(Even-numbered pages are always printed on the back of odd-numbered pages, so page 22 is always printed on the back side of page 21.)

May 4

On your last several spelling tests, you received grades of 88%, 92%, 80%, and 100%. You forgot to study for the most recent test and received a grade of 55%. What is your average?

(The average is 83%.)

August 29

Vicky is buying a new appliance. The salesperson tells her that if she makes a downpayment of $100, she can split the remaining cost evenly over 12 months. If the appliance costs $748, how much will the monthly payments be?

(The monthly payments will be $54.)

May 5

While at the circus, you notice that the happy-faced clown is crying. What is making him so sad? Write about his life.

August 28

I will name three letters. List all of the words you can think of that contain those letters in order. Score 1 point for each word that starts with those letters. Score 3 points for words in which those letters appear in the middle or at the end. The letters are *m*, *e*, and *t*.

May 6

Is your kitchen easy for you to use? Is everything you need within reach? Design a dream kitchen and tell how it would add to the quality of your life. Feel free to include handy inventions that have not yet been created.

August 27

I am thinking of a number that is less than 100. It is not divisible by 5. It is greater than 60. It does not have an 8 or a 9 in it, but it is divisible by 9. Its first digit is twice its second digit. What is the number?

(The number is 63.)

May 7

Write a travel brochure for your room. Make it sound like a great place to visit. Think about qualities that make a place interesting and try to find those qualities in your room.

August 26

It's time for a mental math problem. Begin with the smallest 2-digit number in which both numbers are the same. Increase it by ten. Divide by 3. Multiply by 2 and add 3. What is the number?

(The number is 17.)

May 8

Create your own measuring system and design a ruler that can be used to measure in that system. Use the ruler to measure your desk, your paper, your shoe, your pencil, and other items in the room. How tall are you in your new measuring system?

August 25

A shoe is usually worn for protection or warmth.
List as many other uses for a shoe as possible.

*(Possible answers include using a shoe as a jewelry box,
a doorstop, a planter, a hammer, or a bank.)*

May 9

How is a vacuum cleaner like a plastic cast for a broken bone? List as many similarities as you can.

(Answers may include the facts that both can hold something, both can be tubular, and both help people in some way.)

August 24

Eleanor Roosevelt once said, "No one can make you feel inferior without your consent." Write what you think this means.

May 10

A box of computer paper has 3,000 sheets of paper. Each sheet has a tear-off strip containing 22 holes on each side. How many round dots were left at the paper factory from just one box of computer paper? Think of a possible use for those dots.

(132,000 dots were left at the factory. Uses will vary.)

August 23

Because the North won the Civil War, slavery was abolished in the United States. What might have happened if the South had won the war?

May 11

What number(s) between 50 and 100 can be divided evenly by 2 until you reach a quotient of 1? For example, $32 \div 2 = 16 \div 2 = 8 \div 2 = 4 \div 2 = 2 \div 2 = 1$.

(64 is the only number between 50 and 100 that can be divided evenly by 2 until a quotient of 1 is reached.)

August 22

How is a sneaker like a jeep? List as many similarities as possible.

(Answers may include the facts that they both help you get from place to place, they both have parts made from rubber, and they both are used by humans.)

May 12

What would happen if people became taller when they gained weight instead of getting bigger around? List as many possibilities as you can.

August 21

Make as many words as you can, three letters long or longer, from the letters in the word *grasshopper*.

(Possible answers include grass, gas, hope, rope, grape, page, shopper, press, phase, phrase, *and* shore.*)*

May 13

How is a television like a yo-yo? List as many similarities as you possibly can.

(Answers may include the facts that both can entertain, both can be colorful, and both can attract an audience.)

August 20

You have earned $30 to buy your mother a birthday gift. How will you decide what to buy? Will you buy one large gift or several smaller ones? Is there some way to save yourself the cost of wrapping paper, ribbon, and a card?

May 14

See if you can figure out my pattern. What will the next number be in these patterns 88, 77, 66, ___ (*55, subtract 11*); 1, 3, 4, 7, 11, 18, ___ (*29, add the previous two numbers together*).

August 19

You have planned a swimming party. The day of the party is dark and stormy. List five indoor activities that you and your guests can do.

(Possible activities include renting movies, playing cards, playing board games, working jigsaw puzzles, telling ghost stories, or baking something.)

May 15

It's creative storytelling time. I'll give you fifteen words and together we will make up a story that includes all the words. Who would like to volunteer to begin? The words are *cheese, unicorn, grass, chocolate, room, fish, acrobat, Iraq, family, emeralds, books, mystery, vacation, elves,* and *soda.*

August 18

Draw a person using only the shapes of letters of the alphabet. Try to draw your person so that he or she will look different from anyone else's person.

May 16

Create your autobiography, the story of your life, by drawing a picture of important scenes from your life. Pictures might include a baby in a nursery, a toddler with a favorite toy, family scenes, school scenes, and sports scenes.

August 17

Siri wanted to buy a Persian kitten for $100. She had $17 already and her parents agreed to pay her $3 per hour for baby-sitting her three younger brothers. How many hours will Siri have to baby-sit in order to have enough money to buy the kitten?

(She will have to babysit 28 hours.)

May 17

On a school field trip to a radio station, the disk jockey greets you by name and gives you the royal treatment. The other students are not treated this way. You have never seen the disk jockey or the radio station before. Create a logical explanation for this situation.

August 16

See if you can figure out what comes next in these letter patterns: A, D, G, __ (*J, skip 2 letters*); A, C, A, E, A, __ (*G, go up 2 letters from previous letter between A's*) Here is a tricky one! M, T, W, T, F, __, __ (*S, S, letters at the beginning of the names of days of the week*).

May 18

Estimate how many times the measurement around your head will equal your height. What can you use to measure? How close was your estimate to the actual measurement? Compare your total with your classmates' totals.

August 15

You and a group of friends are sitting around a campfire late at night telling ghost stories. What natural things could you hear or see that might scare everyone under those circumstances?

May 19

You have been chosen to select ten items that will go into a time capsule. The capsule will be opened in 500 years. What items will you put in the capsule?

August 14

Imagine that you have eyes on the tips of all your fingers. What would be good about this situation? What would be bad?

May 20

Create a poem entitled "Ten Ways to Eat an Ice-Cream Cone." Remember that not all poems have to rhyme.

August 13

How many different phone numbers (excluding area codes) can you make using only the digits 7 and 8? Remember there are 7 digits in a phone number.

(128 different 7-digit numbers can be created.)

May 21

Make as many words as you can from the letters in the word *disentanglement*. Make your words three letters long or longer.

(Possible words include tangle, lament, distant, mangle, dangle, glee, sent, meant, gentleman, diet, *and* game.*)*

August 12

How is a drinking straw like a thermometer? List as many similarities as you possibly can.

(Possible answers include the facts that both are thin, both are tubular, and both go in the mouth.)

May 22

Using only one piece of notebook paper, create the best model car possible in ___ minutes.

August 11

If you were the head of a company and three of your best employees were late for work every day, what would you do? Think of two different possible solutions.

May 23

List as many uses as you possibly can for an egg.

(Possible uses include using it as a doll's head, a rolling pin, a ball, a decoration, and a meal.)

August 10

Your little sister's new kitten has crawled under the front seat of the family car and will not come out. List all the ways you can think of to get the kitten out.

May 24

Count the number of books in your desk or book bag. Add the number of sharpened pencils with erasers you have. Multiply that sum by 5. Who in the class has the greatest product?

August 9

Using only one piece of paper, construct the best machine possible in ___ minutes.

May 25

How would your kitchen be different without metal? How would it be different without plastic? How would it be different without glass?

August 8

The circus is featuring elephant rides. The elephant can carry six people on its back at one time. There are thirty-six people in line ahead of you. How many rides will take place before it is your turn to ride?

(There will be six rides before it is your turn. 6 x 6 = 36)

May 26

Figure out how old the following presidents were when they died. Pay special attention to the months in which they were born and died. George Washington—born Feb. 22, 1732; died Dec. 14, 1799. John Adams—born Oct. 30, 1735; died July 4, 1826. James Madison—born Mar. 16, 1751; died June 28, 1836.

(Washington–67, Adams–90, Madison–85)

August 7

You have been entrusted with the honor of designing a new dollar bill. Draw your design and be prepared to explain the significance of each feature.

May 27

Use the names of at least five colors to design a crossword puzzle. Make your clues challenging and be sure your spelling is correct.

August 6

There has been a rash of thefts in your neighborhood. Thirteen bicycles have been stolen in a year. One morning, new bicycles are delivered to the doors of people whose bikes were stolen. How many explanations can you think of for this occurrence?

May 28

A club decided to have a walk-a-thon. One member had 5 people pledge 25¢ a mile. The other 4 members had 25 people pledge 13¢ a mile. Each member walked 11 miles during the walk-a-thon. How much money did the club collect?

(1 member x 5 pledges x .25 x 11 miles = $13.75
4 members x 25 pledges x .13 x 11 miles = $143.00
$143.00 + $13.75 = $156.75)

August 5

If every month had 35 days in it, how many days would make up a year? (*420*) How many more days is that than in a regular year? (*55*) If there were 420 days in a year, how old would you be now? (*Students must figure out their ages in days and divide that number by 420. Their ages will decrease.*)

May 29

Laura, Jane, Rhea, and Gail each play a different sport. They play tennis, softball, swimming, and golf. Use these clues to determine who plays which sport. 1. Laura and Jane hit a ball in their sports. 2. Rhea and Jane participate in sports that can be played alone. 3. Laura wears a uniform, but Jane doesn't.

(Laura-softball, Jane-golf, Rhea-swimming, Gail-tennis)

August 4

How would the world change if people did not need to sleep? Think of as many changes as possible.

May 30

Write the word *acorn*. Drop the second and last letters. Add an *e*. Add a *t* in the middle. Double the last letter. Reverse the first two letters. Add a *k* after the *a*, and divide the letters into two words that spell the result of a buried acorn.

(oak tree)

August 3

Create a code in which each letter of the alphabet has a value from 1 through 26, A=1, B=2, etc. Find the number value of your name by adding the numbers. Is your first name worth more than your last name? How much is your full name worth? Which member of your family has the name with the greatest number value?

May 31

I am thinking of a number that is less than 50. Its digits reversed would be in the 60's. Either way it is written, its digits are three numbers apart. What is the number?

(The number is 36.)

August 2

A new organization has asked your parents to donate your family pet to a special Domestic Animal Display because the animal is such a "perfect example of its breed." Your pet will not be returned to you. Write a letter to the organization stating in calm but firm language why they cannot have your pet.

June 1

A small group of Russian children is going to visit your school. The principal has asked you to get 10 or 12 people together to put on a short show for the visitors. Who will you ask to help you? What kind of show will you plan?

August 1

You have just learned that a teacher is moving in with your family for the rest of the year. What problems could this cause? What positive effects might result from having this house guest?

June 2

An anagram is a word or phrase created by rearranging the letters in another word or phrase. For example, *pot* is an anagram of *top*. Find a word that rhymes with a type of metal container and whose anagram is a word that means rest. *(pan–can, nap)* Find a word that rhymes with the name of a common house pet and whose anagram describes a type of dancing. *(pat–cat, tap)*

July 31

You want to tie together two elastic cords. They are attached to opposite sides of a room. You must stretch both cords to make them meet, but even when you stretch one cord as far as it will go, you can't reach the other unstretched cord. You're alone. How can you solve the problem?

(One way is to tie a long string to cord 1, pick up and stretch cord 2, and use the string to stretch cord 1 toward you.)

June 3

At what time do you eat dinner? Take a survey of class dinner times. Create a graph that shows the outcome of your survey.

July 30

It's creative storytelling time. I'll give you fifteen words and you need to make up a story using those words. Who would like to begin the story? The words are *climate, zoo, earth, bathrobe, pineapple, coyote, tomato, guess, fog, splash, breakfast, dozen, fishy, landfill,* and *poetry.*

June 4

In honor of the arrival of summer, you are going to serve a dinner made up of yellow foods. List every yellow food you can think of and then write out your menu. Remember to select a variety of foods.

July 29

Place operational symbols (+, −, x, or ÷) between the numbers in the following equations to make them true.

1.) 9　3　9　7 = 3
2.) 7　7　5　3 = 3
3.) 6　5　3　6 = 4
4.) 9　6　2　9 = 3

(1. +, +, ÷　2. +, −, ÷　3. x, ÷, −　4. x, ÷, ÷)

June 5

In a music store, you find five different prices on C.D.'s. You can pay $5.99, $6.99, $10.99, $12.99, or $16.99. What is the average price of a C.D.?

(The average price is $10.79.)

July 28

Find a word that rhymes with a word that means
carnival, whose homonym means a matched set
of two, and whose anagram is a means by which
a crop is gathered.

*(**pear**–fair, pair, reap)*

June 6

If you had to live for a week in any public building in the area, where would you live? Why?

July 27

Write a 4 or 5 digit number. Now create another number by reversing the order of the digits in that number. Subtract the smaller number from the larger number. Add the digits in the answer. Then add the digits in that answer, and so on until you have a single digit number. What is that number?

(The answer will always be nine. Example: 7593, 3957, 7593 – 3957 = 3636, 3 + 6 + 3 + 6 = 18, 1 + 8 = 9)

June 7

I will read a set of numbers to you. Place an operation sign (+, −, ÷, or x) between the numbers to make each equation true.

1.) 1 6 5 5 = 7
2.) 3 4 5 8 = 9
3.) 4 7 5 4 = 10
4.) 2 7 3 5 = 8

(1. +, x, +   2. x, +, −   3. +, −, +   4. +, ÷, +)

July 26

New carpet for an apartment costs $555. If the carpet costs $18.50 per yard, how many yards were used? (*30 yards*) How much would it cost to carpet a larger apartment that requires 90 yards of carpet? (*It would cost $1665.*)

June 8

What do you think will be your biggest problem when you are a senior citizen? Is there anything you can do now to prevent that problem? What can people your age do to make life better for some senior citizens?

July 25

Two students have started a window washing business. They clean windows and screens on single-story homes for $2.50 per window. Each house averages 11 windows and the students do 2 houses during an 8-hour day. How much money do they make during an average day?

(They make a total of $55.00 a day.)

June 9

Design and draw the fanciest pair of dark glasses you can. Now create an advertising piece that encourages people to buy those glasses. Remember to choose your vocabulary carefully.

July 24

An automobile dealer sells cars and trucks. On the first day of the month, he had 150 cars and 80 trucks in inventory. By the end of the first week, he had sold 40 cars and 15 trucks from inventory, but he received a shipment of 60 cars and 20 trucks. How many cars and trucks are now in inventory?

(170 cars and 85 trucks)

June 10

How much dirt is there in a round hole which is six inches deep and one foot in diameter? *(There is no dirt—it is a hole.)* Can you think of any other tricky questions?

July 23

In a twenty-four hour day, if a clock struck one time at 1 o'clock, two times at 2 o'clock, and so on until the twenty-fourth hour when it struck twenty-four times, how many times would the clock strike in a twenty-four hour period?

(It would strike 300 times.)

June 11

How is a neighbor like a roach? List as many similarities as you possibly can.

(Possible answers include the facts that they both eat food, they both are alive, and they both live near humans.)

July 22

Arrange these digits, 1, 2, 3, 4, 5, 6, and 7, into an addition problem so that they add up to 100.

```
  +
 100
```

(Possible answers include 24 + 76, 26 + 74, and 53 + 47.)

June 12

List all the places or items in the classroom that have numbers printed on or in them. Look closely. (Examples: clock, computer, #2 pencils, calendar) See if you can find more than twenty-five places or items.

July 21

Using only four of the following numerals, create the largest number and the smallest number possible: 6,7,9,3,1,5, and 4.

(largest number is 9,765; smallest number is 1,345)

June 13

Mance is making yo-yos to earn money to take on his vacation. His yo-yo parts cost $1.78 per yo-yo. Paint costs 22¢ per yo-yo. Mance sells the yo-yos for $3.25 each. How many yo-yos will he have to sell to earn fifty dollars?

($1.78 + $.22 = $2.00—cost of materials per yo-yo
$3.25 - $2.00 = $1.25—profit per yo-yo 50 ÷ 1.25 = 40)

July 20

An anagram is a word or phrase created by changing the order of the letters in another word or phrase. Form anagrams from the following words: *lemons, swore, deal, sink, arches,* and *teach.*

(solemn, worse, lead, skin, search, *and* cheat.)

June 14

(Be sure the U.S. flag is not visible during this activity.) Today is Flag Day. Add the number of red stripes on the flag *(7)* to the number of stars on the flag *(50)*. Then multiply by the number of white stripes *(6)*. Finally add the total number of points on all of the stars on the flag *(250)*. What is the result? *(592)*

July 19

You have accidentally made plans to do things with several people on the same afternoon. You are supposed to look for coins with a metal detector with your mom, roller skate with a friend, and exercise with your dad. How can you solve your scheduling problem?

(One solution would be to ask Mom, Dad, and your friend to put on roller skates and look for coins with you.)

June 15

Ice-cream bars cost 49¢ each. A package of 6
bars costs $2.80. A package of 12 bars costs
$4.89. Imagine that you want to buy *exactly* 34 ice-
cream bars. What would be the cheapest way to
purchase them? How much would they cost?

*(The cheapest way to buy 34 bars is to buy 2 boxes of 12,
1 box of 6, and 4 individual bars. It would cost $14.54)*

July 18

How many televisions do you have in your house? How many color televisions do you have? How many black-and-white televisions? Take a class survey about televisions. Think of a creative way to show the results of your survey.

June 16

What would happen if all automobiles were electric and could only run for two hours without being recharged? List as many possibilities as you can.

July 17

How many hours are there in the months of June, July, and August?

(There are 2,208 hours.)

June 17

See if you can figure out my number patterns.
What will be the next number in these patterns?

1, 101, 2, 102, ___ (*3*)

100, 95, 100, 105, 200, 195, 200, ___ (*205*)

1, 8, 4, 11, 7, ___ (*14*)

July 16

You wake up one morning to find that everything in the world is blue. What problems does this cause?

June 18

What would be the worst thing about not having electricity? What might be some good things about the situation?

July 15

Use the names of at least five states to design a crossword puzzle. Make your clues challenging and spell the words carefully.

June 19

Draw a circle in the top left-hand corner of your paper. Draw a square in the middle. Draw two open half circles at the bottom of the page. Now connect all these figures to create a picture. Don't worry if you don't consider yourself an artist. Just be ready to explain what your picture is.

July 14

Draw plans for building a pair of stilts. Make a shopping list of items you will need to make them. What would you be able to do with stilts that you couldn't do without them?

June 20

Jacob told Mark, his best friend, about something bad that was going to happen. It was a secret. Mark realized that someone could get hurt if the event happened. What could Mark do to solve the situation without betraying his friend?

July 13

Is the sum of an odd and an even number even or odd? Is the sum of two even numbers even or odd? Is the sum of two odd numbers even or odd? Experiment and find out!

(odd + even = odd; even + even = even; odd + odd = even)

June 21

I will give you a sequence of letters. List all of the words that you can think of that contain these letters in order. You will score 1 point for words that begin with these letters, and 3 points for words that have these letters in the middle or at the end. The letters are *q*, *u*, and *a*.

July 12

Using the tips of your fingers to practice, create a new dance that is different from any dances you know. Create directions for the new dance by writing descriptions and drawing outlines of tiny dancing feet.

June 22

Let's do some math magic! Write a number. Multiply it by 100. Add 36. Subtract your original number from that number. Remove 1 digit from that number. Write down the number you remove. Add all the remaining digits together. Subtract that total from its next highest multiple of nine. What is your answer? It should be the number that you omitted and wrote down earlier.

July 11

What might happen if babies were born walking and talking?

June 23

Write the word *presents*. Replace the vowels with *i*'s. Delete the *s*'s. Replace the *p* with a *b*. Exchange the second and third letter. Delete the fourth and fifth letters and add an *h*. Now add the word that means the opposite of *night*.

(The final word is birthday.*)*

July 10

You are shopping with your younger brother when his untied shoelace becomes caught in a moving escalator. Your brother's sneaker is being pulled closer and closer to the metal teeth of the escalator. What can you do to help him? What would you say to him afterwards?

June 24

When you arrive home from school, you find hot water in the bathtub, a radio playing, and no one in the house. List several explanations for this.

July 9

Create a cartoon character out of numbers. Either use a number as a starting point for a character or create a character by combining several numbers. Create a name for your numerical character.

June 25

While camping in the woods, you and a friend become lost. You cannot find the campsite. You have two candy bars and one canteen of water. What plans will you make for survival?

July 8

How is a raft like a tent? List as many similarities as possible.

(Possible answers include the facts that both are used outdoors, both can have wooden parts, both can have canvas parts, and both are used by people.)

June 26

List as many ways as possible for someone your
age to earn money.

July 7

Design your own business card. Place your name in large interesting letters in the center of a 2" x 3" piece of paper. Then add other important information.

June 27

Lillian Hellman, a famous playwrite, once said, "I cannot and will not cut my conscience to fit this year's fashions." What does this quotation mean to you?

July 6

Sue, Bob, Jeff, and Mary raked leaves for Mrs. Guthrie for three hours. She paid them a total of $15.00 for the job. If they split the money evenly, how much did each child earn? (*$3.75*) How much did each child earn per hour? (*$1.25*)

June 28

List as many uses as you possibly can for a wooden block.

(Possible answers include using it as a paperweight, a building block, a doorstop, or a hammer.)

July 5

Imagine that you have just won a contest. The prize is $5,000. The requirements of winning are that you cannot save the money, and you must decide how you will spend it in the next five minutes. Start making your decision now.

June 29

Which contain more days—the first six months of the year or the second six months?

(The first six months contain 181 or 182 days. The second six months contain 184 days.)

July 4

Your town is having a parade. Main Street is two miles long. You are asked to order enough flags to place them every 20 feet along both sides of Main Street. How many flags will you order? Remember there are 5,280 feet in a mile.

(1,056 flags should be ordered.)

June 30

A company has four employees. One earns $8.00 per hour, one earns $8.70 per hour, one earns $11.95 per hour, and one earns $14.70 per hour. If all of the employees worked 39 hours during a week, how much did the company pay in salaries that week?

($312 + $339.30 + $466.05 + $573.30 = $1,690.65)

July 3

You have been helping the little girl next door to create a terrarium out of a large plastic soda bottle. Neither of you has money to buy plants for the terrarium. What are five things you could do to solve this problem?

July 1

What is your favorite color? Take a survey of your classmates' favorite colors. Display your survey results in some way.

July 2

Write ten ingredients that you think would make up the best sandwich in the world.